HOLOCAUST MEMORIES
Speaking the Truth

ELAINE LANDAU

IN THEIR OWN VOICES

FRANKLIN WATTS
A Division of Grolier Publishing
New York London Hong Kong Sydney
Danbury, Connecticut

When I was about four or five I sometimes played with a Christian girl. She lived down the street. She was about two or three years older than me, but we got along very well. We were good friends. One day I happened to mention that I was Jewish. She didn't react one way or another. It didn't seem

Frontis: *Visitors remember the people of the Holocaust at an Auschwitz crematorium.*

Interior design by Molly Heron
Cover photograph ©: Hulton Getty/Liaison Agency.

Photographs ©: Courtesy of the survivors and their families: 21, 34, 50, 56, 59, 70, 76, 87, 89; AP/Wide World Photos: 83 (Alik Keplicz), 27, 40, 55, 73, 75; Archive Photos: 43; Corbis-Bettmann: 12 (UPI), 38, 52, 67; FPG International: 15; Hulton Getty/Liaison Agency, Inc.: 6, 10, 13, 22, 29, 33, 39, 48, 53, 63; Liaison Agency, Inc.: 81 (Piotr Malecki), 78, 84 (Krzysztof Wojcik); National Archives at College Park: 24; United States Holocaust Memorial Museum/Dokumentationsarchiv des Oesterreichischen Widerstandes: 46, 60, 62.

Visit Franklin Watts on the Internet at:
http://publishing.grolier.com

Library of Congress Cataloging-in-Publication Data

Holocaust memories: speaking the truth/ [compiled] by Elaine Landau.
    p. cm.
Includes bibliographical references (p.) and index.
ISBN 0-531-11742-1
    1. Holocaust, Jewish (1939–1945)—Personal narratives—Juvenile literature.
[1. Holocaust, Jewish (1939–1945)—Personal narratives.] I. Landau, Elaine.

D804.195 .H68 2000+
940.53'18—dc21   00-032511

CONTENTS

When I was about four or five I sometimes played with a Christian girl. She lived down the street. She was about two or three years older than me, but we got along very well. We were good friends. One day I happened to mention that I was Jewish. She didn't react one way or another. It didn't seem

INTRODUCTION

ADOLF HITLER, the infamous German dictator, earned a place in history for all the wrong reasons. Ruling Germany from 1933 to 1945, he was responsible for the death of more innocent civilians than any other leader in modern times. Hitler's rise to power began humbly enough. After Germany's World War I defeat, he became the leader of a small group of people known as Nazis. The Nazis promised the German citizens, who were discouraged and resentful after losing the war, that they would lead the nation from defeat to the glory that was once Germany's.

At first, many people refused to take Hitler and the Nazis seriously. They considered Hitler an extremist who was unlikely to attract a strong following—but they couldn't have been more wrong. Hitler proved to be a charismatic speaker

Adolf Hitler

with the uncanny ability to stir a crowd emotionally. He was also a shrewd politician and an excellent organizer who managed to influence an entire nation.

Hitler promised revenge for Germany's defeat by Great Britain, France, Russia, and the United States. He planned the unification of Germany and Austria—a union that was forbidden by the treaty that ended World War I. He then intended to fight four wars—one against Czechoslovakia; a second against Great Britain and France; a third against Russia; and a fourth against the United States. After his *anschluss* (unification) policy was politically defeated, he invaded Austria on March 12, 1938. Then he tried to begin the first of his planned wars, against Czechoslovakia, but negotiated for land instead.

In 1939, Great Britain and France decided that they would declare war on Germany if Hitler invaded another country. He invaded Poland on September 1 of that year, and World War II began. The Russian Army then defeated the German forces that were attacking Russia.

Hitler's intention was to enlarge his domain. However, he had another plan—to keep Germany and the places he conquered "racially pure." That is, to rid the world of the Jews, Gypsies, and other groups Hitler regarded as inferior. He called his plan the New Order. It emphasized military service and national pride and condemned Jews and other minorities to death. To make sure the New Order would be accepted, the Nazis saturated newspapers, films, and radio broadcasts with propaganda endorsing Hitler's message and methods. The resulting mass murder of six million Jews and millions of others, including Gypsies, Slavs, Communists, and homosexuals became known as the Holocaust.

While there wasn't sufficient international resistance to prevent the Holocaust, eventually a number of nations banded together to halt Hitler's territorial aggression. The United States, Great Britain, Russia, and France were known as the Allies in this struggle. They opposed the countries that unified to form the Axis forces: Germany, Italy, and Japan. As World War II progressed, other nations sided with either the Allies or the Axis.

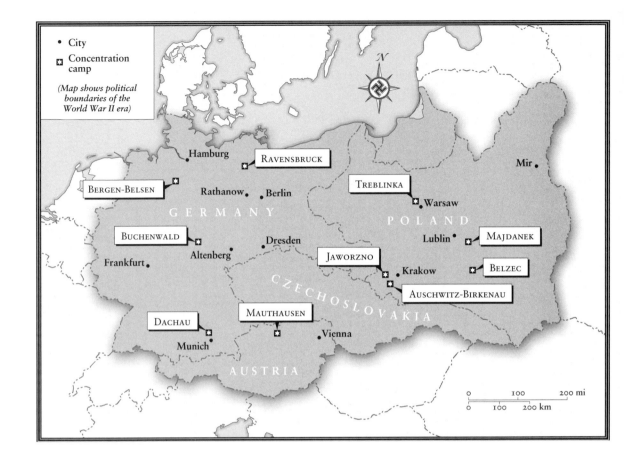

In May 1945 Germany surrendered. Hitler had committed suicide the previous week. The dictator was dead, but the aftermath of the horror he created lives on.

This is a book about the Holocaust. It combines the thoughts, memories, and voices of people who in one way or another were affected by that dreadful time. Most of these individuals experienced the Holocaust itself and survived Hitler's regime. This book creates a picture of a past whose dismal reality cannot be denied.

Chapter One
FRANK MOSES

FRANK MOSES and his family left Germany in 1939. The war hadn't broken out yet, but Hitler's anti-Semitic (Jewish discrimination) propaganda had begun to take root in the minds and hearts of many Germans. The lives of German Jews would soon be turned upside down. Even very small children felt the sting of the changing attitudes around them:

When I was about four or five, I sometimes played with a Christian girl. She lived down the street. She was about two or three years older than me, but we got along very well. We were good friends. One day I happened to mention that I was Jewish. She didn't react one way or another. It didn't seem to matter to her. As always, that day we parted friends.

9

This tailor's shop was defaced with many anti-Semitic slogans. Graffiti like this was spread all over the cities long before World War II broke out.

A few days later I was outside playing again when the same girl came over and kicked one of my toys into the gutter. That child looked at me with such hatred and screamed, "You dirty Jew!" I was shocked and hurt. I knew that my life was going to change.

Frank Moses's life changed drastically, as did the lives of his family. He described what life was like for his father:

My father suffered also. He had a lot of non-Jewish friends. He used to play cards with them. He drank beer with them. He always felt close to these people. By 1936, none of them would even speak to him. When they saw my father, they would cross the street and look at him with contempt. My father never understood how they could be that way. They had always gotten along in the past.

It didn't take Frank's family long to realize that there was no future for Jews in Hitler's Germany. They knew that they had to leave the country, but it wouldn't be easy. The Moses family needed to find a country willing to take them, and at the time there were long lines of Jews at the door of every foreign consulate in Berlin.

Nevertheless, the Moseses were determined to relocate safely. They became friendly with some people at the Chilean consulate in Berlin. Frank's parents thought they might go to a Spanish-speaking country, so they asked the consulate to recommend some tutors to help them learn the language. Some of the staff there wanted to earn extra money, and the family paid them generously. Frank was fortunate that his family owned a number of department stores and was wealthy. The Spanish lessons progressed, and the tutors and students became good friends. "Through the tutoring lessons we made a connection with those people. We were no longer

Many Jewish families left Germany at the beginning of the war. The Nazis in the background of this photograph taunt the family as they flee in terror.

just one of thousands of families hoping to escape the Nazis," said Frank.

Before the family went anywhere, however, they were forced to endure *Kristallnacht* (Crystal Night, or the Night of Broken Glass), which took place on November 9, 1938. That night, members of the Nazi Party attacked Jewish homes, businesses, and synagogues throughout Germany and

A worker in Berlin cleans broken glass out of a Jewish shop the day after *Kristallnacht*.

Austria. The windows of Jewish-owned shops were shattered. Synagogues were vandalized and set on fire. Dozens of Jews were murdered that night and approximately thirty thousand were arrested. Frank Moses's father was among those taken into custody and sent to a Nazi concentration camp.

Frank's family lived in Rathanow, near one of their stores, but Frank was visiting his grandmother in Berlin when the attack happened. He was only seven then but he recalls Crystal Night:

My grandmother had her driver take us around the city to see the damage. It was dangerous because there was still broken glass everywhere. It's a miracle that the car's tires weren't punctured. We saw the synagogues in flames. My grandmother was crying. She became especially upset when we reached the downtown area and she saw all the special landmarks she loved in ruins. The Jewish-owned bakeries, candy stores, restaurants, and theaters were destroyed. In some cases, Jews had owned businesses in partnership with non-Jews. These were all destroyed too.

The Nazis were intent on sending out a clear message to anyone who chose to do business—or even associate—with Jews.

After we returned, we called Rathanow. We were anxious to know if my family was all right. That's when we learned that the Nazis took my father. My mother tried everything to get him released. She went to the people we knew at the Chilean Consulate. They felt sorry for us and consoled my mother. They tried very hard to get visas for us. If we presented those, we hoped my father would be released and we could leave Germany.

The lower-level members of the Nazi party tended to be easily impressed with official-looking documents. Before Hitler's campaign against the Jews went into high gear, Jews with visas from other countries were often permitted to leave.

It took about seven months before our papers finally came through. My mother immediately presented the visas

These agents at Gestapo headquarters receive reports of suspected rebels from Nazi secret policemen.

at Gestapo* headquarters, and they let my father go. When we first saw him we barely recognized him. He had been through so much and it showed. He had on the same suit he was wearing the day he was arrested. Seven months and they never even gave him a prison uniform. He wore that suit all day, and he had to sleep in it too.

The sanitary conditions at the camp where he was held had been terrible. When he returned, his whole body was covered with boils, and he smelled miserably. When my mother opened the door and saw him standing there in that condition, she was heartbroken.

At least my father came home. His brother Karl, who was taken by the Nazis at the same time, died at the camp. Jews in Nazi camps would usually keep very quiet and stay out of sight to avoid being beaten by the guards. My Uncle Karl would always joke and laugh. One day a guard saw him doing this and began beating him. He beat my uncle so ferociously that he had a heart attack and died soon afterward. All this happened in front of my father, but he wasn't able to help his own brother. If he had interfered, he would have been killed too.

I lost between 30 and 40 percent of my family during the Holocaust. That percentage is low due to my family's wealth and influence, which enabled us to leave Germany. Families who were poor, who couldn't afford an expensive

*The Nazi secret police force known for its brutality

16

move to a distant country, had to stay in Germany. Of course, they died.

If you were a Jew while Hitler was in power, it didn't matter how much you loved your country or how patriotic you were. None of that mattered anymore. My father had served in the German army during World War I. My uncles on my father's side fought bravely for Germany too. One lost a leg and another was blinded in the war. Because of their war injuries, they were unable to get visas to leave Germany once the Nazis were in charge. You needed two things to get a visa—perfect health and money. So ironically, a Jew who lost a leg fighting for Germany was certain to be killed in a German death camp during the Holocaust.

After my father's return we tried to find transportation to Chile. It was difficult. Many people were trying to get out, and all the ships were booked. We finally found a small Italian ship that could take us. My father wanted to buy third-class tickets—he hoped to hold on to the small amount of cash that we could get out of Germany, so we would have some when we arrived in Chile.* But the only cabin left on the ship was a very expensive stateroom. To get out of Germany and save our lives, my father had to take the stateroom. That's what we spent our last bit of money on.

---

*Jews leaving Germany were not permitted to take their valuables with them. The Nazis confiscated their bank accounts, property, jewelry, furs, and other items of value, such as gold or silver candlesticks, expensive paintings, and sculptures.

My grandmother, who had always been wealthy, was coming to Chile with us. We were all going to fly from Germany to Genoa, Italy, where we'd board the ship. My father warned my grandmother not to hide any valuables in the suitcases. We could get into terrible trouble if the German customs agents found them. But my father was in for a surprise.

When we got to the airport, my grandmother looked around and didn't see a certain customs agent. In a very demanding voice she asked, "Where is Herr Muller?" One of the other customs agents was very polite and said he would page Herr Muller over the loudspeaker. Herr Muller came over to us immediately and apologized to my grandmother for not being there. Can you imagine that happening in Nazi Germany in 1939? After searching our bags, he declared that everything was in order and sent us on our way.

When we arrived at our hotel in Genoa, my grandmother opened her suitcase. It was filled with her jewels. She had bribed the customs agent Herr Muller. My father was furious with her. If anything had gone wrong, we wouldn't have been allowed to leave Germany. We would have died in a Nazi death camp. I wouldn't be here to tell the story.

Thankfully, nothing went wrong. It's likely that the other customs agents were also being bribed by Jewish families fleeing the country. So it wouldn't have been in their best interest to report one another. My father felt that my grandmother had taken too great a risk. But we arrived in Santiago, Chile, with money to start a new life.

Frank Moses lived in Chile until he was twenty-seven years old. He became a press photoengraver for a large Chilean newspaper. After coming to the United States, he continued to work as a photoengraver. He got married and had two sons. In reflecting on his life as an American, Frank Moses declared, "The Holocaust will not be forgotten. It's being kept alive through school curricula, the media, Holocaust museums, and memorials. I feel secure in the United States. I know that Crystal Night will never happen here. The Holocaust survivor testimonies will preserve the truth forever."

When I was about four or five I sometimes played with a Christian girl. She lived down the street. She was about two or three years older than me, but we got along very well. We were good friends. One day I happened to mention that I was Jewish. She didn't react one way or another. It didn't seem

Chapter Two
BASIA MANDEL

BASIA MANDEL was born in Poland in 1925. She lived in a region where there were many Jews. More than five generations on her mother's side had come from the area. Basia describes her childhood as happy. Her father was a tailor, and she remembers having lovely dresses to wear and all the food she could eat.

Yet that part of her life became unrecognizable after 1939 when Germany invaded Poland, and Hitler's campaign against the Jews swung into action. Jews were soon herded into a separate section of the city known as the ghetto. Six months later there was a fence and armed guards surrounding it. No one was allowed out of the ghetto unless they were serving as forced labor for the German government or

Basia Mandel as a child with her mother

German manufacturers. In those instances, the workers were escorted to and from work by the guards.

Seventeen-year-old Basia was among those pressed into this Nazi version of slave labor, but at the time she was considered fortunate to be alive. The Nazi goal was ultimately to kill everyone in the ghetto, so Jews were periodically rounded up and shipped out to death camps. No one was safe. Basia, her parents, and her fiancé, Meier, all knew it was only a matter of time before it was their turn. Rounding the Jews up gradually was the Nazis' way of emptying the ghetto while exploiting Jewish workers for as long as they could.

Many young people, including Basia, were forced to work for the Nazis. These children are being prepared to work at a labor camp in Poland.

Jews could only hope to avoid being transported to death camps or taken out to a nearby location and shot. Basia's father was part of a group of people who were arbitrarily rounded up, driven to a wooded area on the city's outskirts, and killed. As time passed, the Nazis developed more "sophisticated" techniques for the mass murder of Jews for what became known as Hitler's "final solution." Bullets were needed for war so it was considered inefficient to use them. Nevertheless, what happened to Basia's father was not uncommon during the early years of the war. Basia describes a similar instance:

Once a large group of Jews were brought to our town. The Nazis put them in our shul.* It used to be such a beautiful shul, but the Nazis took it over for their purposes. The Jews were only there for about two or three hours. Then the Nazis took them out and shot them in the woods by a lake. The Nazis left the bodies in a ditch they had the victims dig. The ground was so soaked with blood that it seeped into the lake. The lake was turning red with blood. The bodies had to be dug up and buried in another place. I saw it. The Nazis made other Jewish men do the work.

Within their limited sphere of options, Jews did what they could to survive. Some built bunkers—secret hiding places

---

*A Jewish house of worship

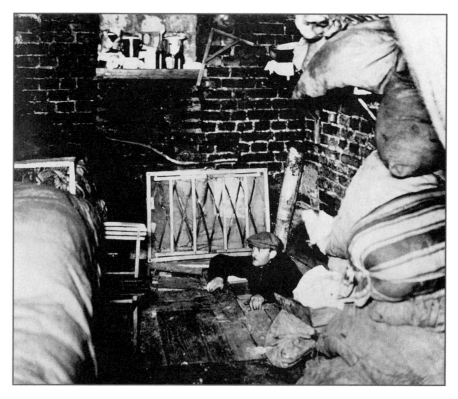

A Jewish man is forced to leave his bunker.

within the ghetto. Meier, Basia's fiancé, built two underground tunnels to protect his family and Basia's. One of the bunkers led to a sewer from which it was possible to get to a lake. The other led to the back wall of the ghetto. As anticipated, the bunkers proved essential during wide-scale roundups that threatened the residents' survival. Ghetto residents who had bunkers fled to them to escape the Nazis. Basia describes what happened:

The Nazis found the bunker leading to the sewer. All the people had to come out or be killed on the spot. My mother and fiancé were among those hiding there. The Nazis herded the people into the street. They had to wait out there for one and a half days without food or water. Anyone caught moving was shot. They took the people to the railroad and put them in cattle cars. My mother took that train to Auschwitz.* It was the end. They killed her there.

Somehow my fiancé escaped. He came back to the second bunker. I was there with four other people. The Nazis hadn't found us, but they did something almost as bad. When they found the bunker my mother and fiancé were in they pushed the debris used to conceal it on our bunker. We were trapped inside. We were there for a day and a half. I think we could have died in there. There was hardly any air left to breathe.

My fiancé came back to where he thought our bunker was. It was too covered with debris for even him to easily recognize. He called out to see where we were. We knew his voice right off. We weren't scared because we knew it wasn't the Nazis coming back for us. We yelled back, and he found us. He dug us out. He saved us all that time, but I was the only one of the four in that bunker who survived the war.

---

*A Nazi death camp

After finding us, my fiancé went to look for his parents. They never made it to a bunker, but they were all right. Meier's parents were always good to me. His mother told me I would survive when I was sure I wouldn't. My mother had told me the same thing before she was killed. When I asked her who would save me, she said Meier would. Now Meier's mother insisted that I marry her son while we were in the ghetto.

I had always dreamed of a wedding with my family. I wanted a beautiful ceremony. But now those dreams were gone. My parents were already dead. Meier's mother kept saying, "I feel that you will survive. You have to do me a favor. The Nazis will kill me, and I'll never see my grandchildren, so marry Meier now. Make sure our family goes on." I did what she asked. I loved Meier. I loved his family too.

Meier's father did not live to see the wedding. He died of typhus three weeks beforehand. There was no medicine and very little food in the ghetto, and occupants died of sickness and starvation daily. People in the ghetto couldn't give their dead loved ones a proper burial. Bodies were taken out to the street, where they were later picked up in wagons and heaped into mass graves. Meier's mother wanted more than that for Meier's father. Even though they were not permitted out of the ghetto after dark, some friends helped them secretly carry his body to a nearby Jewish cemetery.

"The others left. My future mother-in-law and I dug a

There were very few supplies in the Jewish ghettos. People waited on long lines to pump water from the wells.

shallow grave for him with our bare hands," says Basia. The women worked quickly while it was still dark. There was no religious service, so they arrived back in the ghetto before morning. Basia and Meier married soon afterward. Basia describes the circumstances:

Our local rabbi was dead. He was killed in the first action. So a shochet, a person who makes sure that chickens are butchered according to Jewish dietary laws, performed the ceremony. He had religious training so he did the service. We didn't have a chupa,* so they held a blanket over us. We were married for over fifty-three years. Meier died in my arms a year ago. When he was in his coffin I said to him, "Your funeral was nicer than our wedding." So you can imagine the wedding.

In August 1943, the Germans decided to close down the ghetto or make it Juden-free. That meant empty of Jews, but it also meant much more than that. It meant our lives. The Nazis made an announcement over the loudspeakers. Mothers with young children were ordered to line up outside. They were told to bring their babies. The Nazis took the babies from their mothers and threw them in cattle cars. The smallest ones were put in sacks and suffocated. One woman I knew refused to give them her two toddlers. The soldiers pulled the children over to a

---

*A covering under which Jewish couples are wed

sewer and threw them down it. They shot the mother on the spot. The other mothers were lined up and machine-gunned. After the women were killed, the Jewish men were forced to bury them in mass graves. I saw this with my own eyes. This I will never forget.

Prisoners are forced to bury fellow Jews in mass graves while being supervised by Nazi soldiers.

With the ghetto being cleared out, it wasn't safe for us to hide there anymore. We decided to hide in the woods on the outskirts of town—at least until things settled down. My husband, his mother, his brother, and I would go. Some others from the ghetto came too. Meier had gotten hold of a rifle. He made contact with a Christian engineer he used to work for. Meier's old boss gave him ammunition for the gun. We would need it for what was ahead.

The group separated when they reached the woods. It was unrealistic to think a group that size could hide safely. There was the ever-present danger of being discovered by the Ukrainian soldiers that the Germans hired to help eliminate the Jews. Basia was ill when the group started out, and her condition worsened as the days passed. Desperate for help, Meier brought her to the home of the former employer who had provided him with ammunition. Basia explains:

I was so sick from eating unripened vegetables all the time. We were in hiding, and that's all we could get. When we hid in the ghetto, Meier would sneak out at night to bring them back for us. In the woods, it was hard to find anything to eat. The Christian engineer and his wife took me in until I got better. The wife was an angel. She treated me so kindly. After about a week Meier came to get me. I was better, but I still couldn't walk very well. Most of the time Meier had to carry me.

I still hadn't completely recovered when we were

spotted by some Ukrainian soldiers. They shot at us, and Meier shot back. We had to run to get away. I was too sick to run so Meier ran as best he could while carrying me. We escaped, but Meier's mother and brother were killed by soldiers. Meier found their bodies in the woods while he was looking for food.

Basia and Meier hid in the woods for another five months. They knew that they could be captured or killed at any time. The couple agreed that if they were discovered and had to separate to escape, they would meet up at a specific bunker in the former Jewish ghetto. They hoped that by then it would be safe to go back. The Nazi presence there was likely to have diminished since the ghetto had been cleared out. Eventually, their plan was put into action.

We were spotted again and shot at. We had to run in different directions. I lost my balance on a steep cliff and rolled down it. I landed near a lake and hid behind some bushes. I stayed there until it was night. I did not know where to go. I was completely lost, and it had started to rain. I was drenched, but I kept on walking. I saw a church. I was desperate, so I took a chance and knocked on the door.

Some nuns answered it. They looked at me and knew I was Jewish, but they decided to help me. They took me in that rainy night and hid me for nearly a week. This placed them at great risk, and they were afraid to let me stay *longer.* * *The nuns dressed me in a nun's habit before I left and pointed me in the direction of the old Jewish ghetto. I had to make it back. If Meier was still alive, I would find him there.*

As I walked, I carried a crucifix the nuns had given me. To get to the ghetto, I had to go over a bridge and past Gestapo headquarters on the other side of the bridge. It started to rain again. I saw a soldier by the bridge. I passed him. Nobody stopped me—I just walked on. I kept thinking about what my mother and mother-in-law had said. They knew I was going to survive. Now I thought that maybe they were right. Maybe it was some kind of prophecy or something. The feeling didn't last long. I was almost at the ghetto when a man from the Gestapo saw me. He knew right away that I wasn't a nun. He must have realized that a nun wouldn't be heading for the ghetto. He started shouting and shooting. I ran, but a bullet hit me in the leg. It was just a flesh wound, and I was able to get away.

I made it to the bunker where I was supposed to meet Meier. He was there waiting for me. There were also others hiding there. Meier helped everyone. He left the bunker at night to scavenge for food and other things we needed. He took a lot of risks, and sometimes I was afraid he wouldn't

---

*Christians who helped Jews suffered serious consequences if discovered by the Nazis. They were often sent to Nazi death camps themselves. In the nuns' case, there could have been repercussions for the convent and church.

come back. The Nazis were always on the lookout for Jews. There were fifteen of us in that bunker. One was a year-and-a-half-old girl. All of us survived—we wouldn't have without Meier.

The year was 1944. We didn't know very much about what was going on outside the bunker. One day we heard a lot of commotion from the outside. Then we heard Russian being spoken. We knew that the Germans were gone, and the Russian soldiers were here. It was finally safe to leave the bunker. Meier went out first. The soldiers told him to stay inside until they cleared the ground. Before leaving, the Germans had scattered landmines all over.

Warsaw was left in ruins after the end of the war. The Nazis destroyed the entire ghetto and most of its inhabitants.

They got us out soon afterwards. Our rescuer was a Russian Jewish soldier. He understood what we'd been through. He hugged us and brought us food and water. I could barely open my eyes. I had been in the dark bunker for so long that the sunlight hurt. I couldn't believe we were free, that we had really survived. Yet it was true— the war was over and we were safe.

Basia and Meier lived in both Italy and Israel. Later they emigrated to the United States. Basia enjoyed her life with

Basia Mandel and her husband, Meier, recently visited Israel. Here, they pose with a statue of the first prime minister of Israel, David Ben-Gurion.

Meier in the United States. They had two daughters, who also had two daughters each. Today one of Basia's greatest joys is spending time with her four grandchildren. She also cherishes the time she spends at her synagogue. Years after the war, on a return visit to Israel, Basia and Meier met the woman who was once the year-and-a-half-old girl with them in the bunker. She had married, had two sons, and was living in Israel. Basia and Meier also kept in touch with the Christian engineer until the time of his death.

Chapter Three
BIANCA LERNER

BIANCA LERNER was born in Warsaw in 1929. Her mother was a pediatrician; her father was a successful businessman. In many ways, Bianca considered her childhood ideal.

I was a very lucky little girl. I lived in a beautiful home. My parents exposed me to all kinds of cultural things. I participated in sports and traveled extensively. I went to private school. I was the only Jewish girl there, but I wasn't discriminated against. My parents had Gentile [non-Jewish] friends. Warsaw was very integrated, unlike the shtetls.* It

---

*A small rural Jewish village

36

was a cosmopolitan city. As a matter of fact, Warsaw was known as the Paris of eastern Europe.

I was very pampered. My mother always protected me. That was the mother–doctor in her. No doctors should take care of their children. They drive you crazy with their concern. So that was my prewar life. I didn't realize I was privileged at the time. Later, I realized it.

My father knew that we should get out of Poland even before the Nazis arrived. He was a very smart man and had all kinds of contacts. We were supposed to leave in October 1939, but the war began in September of that year. Our planned departure had been one month too late. We never got out.

Germany's invasion of Poland changed everything for Bianca Lerner's family. Her father had been in the Polish army reserves. He was now called to the front of the line to fight as Poland tried to halt the German occupation. Warsaw, which had once been a center for culture and the arts, suddenly became a war zone. The Germans bombed the city night and day. Bianca described her experiences:

My father had to go to the front. My mother and I were in Warsaw during the bombing. They were bombing constantly. We lived in a beautiful apartment building, but we had to leave because it was bombed. We went to my aunt's home where we stayed in the cellar. But the bombs continued. I remember running from house to house. My

At the beginning of the war, German bombs destroyed many parts of the city of Warsaw.

father was still away. I was with my mother and aunt. The city was on fire. There were bodies everywhere.

It took about a month for the Germans to capture Poland. The bombing was finally over. My father walked back from the front. He found my mother and me. We went to his office. He had chocolate and sardines there, so that's what we ate. We were lucky to have any food.

There were horses running wild in the streets. People were catching them and killing them for food, but my father always loved horses. So when someone we knew offered us some horse meat, my father couldn't eat it. He just couldn't bring himself to do it.

With the Germans in Warsaw, the lives of all the Jewish residents changed dramatically. Jews were no longer permitted to own businesses, and Jewish children could not attend school. Before long, Jews were required to wear armbands with the Star of David on them, and they were herded into a sectioned-off part of the city, which became known as the

Jews wearing the required armbands in the streets of Warsaw

This wall separated the Warsaw Ghetto from the rest of the city.

Warsaw Ghetto. Despite their circumstances, Bianca's father still had some money left and tried to make his daughter's life as normal as possible. She describes his efforts:

My father hired some teachers for different subjects. There was a man who taught me English, and a woman who taught me French. I don't know of any other people who did things like that for their children. They lacked the foresight and the financial means.

My father also wanted me to be busy with something so I wouldn't think about how things were. So he got me a rabbit. I don't know how he managed to do this. He just wanted to make my life as normal as possible. But things could never be normal.

My mother worked at a clinic in the ghetto. The doctors there didn't offer very much help. And there was an atmosphere of fear all around us. Every time my parents left our apartment, I was afraid I'd never see them again.

In the beginning, the Germans gave us rations, but they were not enough to survive on. There was a black market in the ghetto. Young boys would sneak out of the ghetto and bring food and other things back. Sometimes they were caught by the Germans and shot, but some got away with it. If you had money, you could buy things.

Bianca saw numerous children living alone in the ghetto. Their parents had been killed by the Nazis. She was concerned about the hungry children around her, and though she was just a child herself, Bianca thought of a way to help.

A man in the ghetto had a cow, and I knew he needed food for the cow. So I went to everybody to collect their potato peelings. I brought them to this man and told him that I would give him the potato peels for his cow if he would give me some milk. He agreed and everyday for a while I had fresh milk to give to the children. I also asked people to give a little bread or anything else they could spare. That way I had some food to give the children too.

Yet Bianca knew that her efforts could not make a significant difference. She continues:

I was in the ghetto for over three years. I saw people shot for no reason. Of course, for the Germans there was a reason—they were Jewish. People would be taken out of the ghetto and sent to death camps. Many starved to death. I saw the emaciated bodies of young children stacked on wheelbarrows. You would walk around the ghetto and see bodies in the street. You couldn't do anything about it. You were dehumanized.

As a pediatrician, my mother still did whatever she could to help children. One day someone came to where we lived to ask if my mother would see a very sick little boy in the ghetto. She agreed, but while she was there, German soldiers came in. They took the child, his family, and

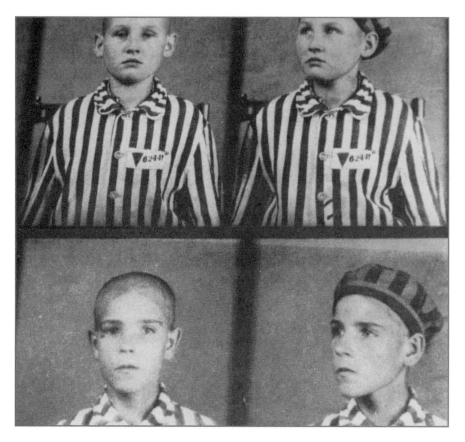

Photos of young victims of Auschwitz concentration camp

everyone in the apartment building, including my mother. They were all put in a cattle car and sent to a death camp.

My mother was a doctor; she had a poison pill with her. I'm hoping she used it—I'll never know. We found out that a sister of hers was on the same train. My mother might have lived longer if she was with her sister. My father and I were devastated.

Bianca might have eventually shared her mother's fate, but to her surprise, she was rescued from the ghetto. She describes how it happened:

When I was in school, I became very friendly with one of the Christian girls there. I would go to her house and she would come to my house. Her father was a doctor like my mother. In any case, my father got in contact with her father. He persuaded him to get me out of the ghetto. My friend's father saved me. I don't know how he did it, but he bribed a guard. The guard sort of looked the other way, and I just walked out of the ghetto. I'm alive by a sheer miracle.

The doctor met me at the stipulated place. He took me home with him. They were wonderful people. I stayed with them for a time. The only problem was that the neighbors knew me, and some of their relatives knew me. So when they were around or when anyone rang the bell, I had to hide in the closet. You couldn't trust anyone.

My father got out of the ghetto too. But it was tremendously hard for him to find a place. Even though he had so many Gentile friends, they were afraid. Finally, one woman with a very elderly mother agreed to help. Her mother was very poor, so she did it for the money. She said that if my father paid, he could hide in a shack her mother had. He was padlocked in that shack most of the time. I visited him there a few times. It was terrible. He was alone there with his thoughts. He kept thinking how things might have been different if only he had planned to leave Poland earlier. He tortured himself thinking about it.

After a few months, hiding in the closet at the doctor's house became very damaging for me psychologically. The doctor decided to place me in an orphanage run by nuns. He had approached the Mother Superior to see if I could be part of the orphanage. Only she and her secretary knew I was Jewish. I later found out that the Mother Superior saved twenty-three Jewish girls. None of us knew about the rest. That way if one was discovered, the others would still be safe.

Being in that convent was quite an experience for me. Before I left his house, the doctor sat down with me and gave me the name Janina Marzec. He explained that the girls at the orphanage came from very poor backgrounds. The doctor told me that I had to fit in. He said that my Polish was too good and that I should try to make some grammatical mistakes. He also told me to say that my father was a carpenter and my mother a peasant woman.

While I was at the convent I had to be an actress even though at times this would be very hard for me. I was very educationally oriented. Everyone in my family was a professional. I had an uncle in Berlin, Germany, who was a lawyer and an aunt who was a Ph.D. But the doctor drilled me on my new identity to make sure I didn't give myself away.

The first crisis at the convent came when I had to go to confession. The doctor had failed to tell me what to do. I

Some of these students could be young Jewish women hiding in the convent school from the Nazis.

realized what might happen if I didn't say the right thing. But I knew that in confession you had to confess, and I knew that anything about sex was taboo. So I told the priest that I had been thinking about boys.

I couldn't ask the Mother Superior what to do. I didn't have access to her. This order was very active and she was often away. She didn't have much contact with the other girls anyway, and she couldn't have made an exception with me. We had to be very careful.

After I was there for a year and a half, the Polish underground forces staged an uprising against the Germans. It was 1944, and I was fourteen years old. I immediately went out and joined the Polish underground. I joined the first unit I found. The nuns let me go. They blessed me and wished me well.

The underground fighters gave me a gun, but they didn't teach me how to use it. I was told to just point and shoot. We were fighting from behind barricades and going from street to street. Of course no one suspected that I was Jewish. The uprising lasted about a month. We had no food or ammunition; in the end we were left with nothing.

My father was a fighter too. He wanted to come to the area where I was, but he was hit by a stray bullet. It wasn't fatal. The bullet lodged in his lung. The underground had set up hospitals in schools—wherever they could place cots. That is where they put my father. There were no supplies or clean sheets. Nothing. It was horrendous. My father sent a message to me letting me know where he was. He signed it "grandmother" because I was supposed to be an orphan. I went to my father—I didn't want to be separated from him.

When the hospital was evacuated I went back to the underground. I was eventually captured and put in a prisoner-of-war camp. A nurse at the hospital betrayed my father. She saw that he was circumcised and realized that he was a Jew. She reported him to the Nazis and they shot him. A few months later the Russians liberated the area. If they had arrived a little earlier my father might have lived.

Jews from the Warsaw Ghetto surrender to German soldiers after the uprising.

The Germans never found out that I was Jewish. They just thought I was a member of the Polish underground, and as their prisoner of war I was moved around to different camps. At one place we were only allowed to relieve ourselves every twenty-four hours. There were German guards marching up and down in front of us all the while. It was dehumanizing. At night in the barracks, we were packed in so tightly that if one out of 200 people turned over, the other 199 also had to. Once a day we were given a slice of bread and a brew made from rotten turnips.

At another camp in the city of Altenburg, the German people living nearby would walk past it and look inside. They looked at us as though we were animals in a zoo. The prisoners were put to work in a factory making bullets for the Germans. Whenever possible, we would sabotage the work, hoping to hurt the German war effort. I was later taken to Bergen-Belsen,* where the Allied forces liberated us in April 1945.

I think I was meant to survive. At the end of the war I was fifteen years old and not in terrible physical condition. I went to a displaced persons' camp.** I didn't want to go back to Poland. The Poles were killing a lot of Jews who returned to claim property, homes, and other possessions.

---

*A Nazi concentration camp

**Camps where homeless survivors went to live temporarily

Bianca Lerner with her daughter today

My parents were dead. There was nothing to go back to now.

Bianca lived in England with an uncle before coming to the United States, which became her permanent home. She married, raised a son and a daughter, and now has a grand-daughter. Today, Bianca enjoys playing bridge, doing embroidery, and perhaps, most importantly, speaking to school and community groups about the Holocaust.

Chapter Four

ALLAN BERK

As HITLER's persecution of the Jews extended throughout much of Europe, it eventually touched the life of Allan Berk, a Jewish teenager living in Czechoslovakia. Some of Allan's family left Czechoslovakia before the Jews were taken from the ghettos there and placed in the Nazi death camps. But Allan was not able to escape. He was among those who rode the cattle cars to Auschwitz-Birkenau, an infamous death camp. Allan describes what it was like:

When you came to the camp, the Nazis decided if you would live a little longer. If you were sent to the right, you lived; if to the left, you died. My mother, sister-in-law, and her small child were gassed right away. My

The entrance to the concentration camp Auschwitz-Birkenau in Poland

brother Sheldon and I had our heads shaved and were given striped uniforms and wooden shoes to wear. After they tattooed numbers on our arms, we went to the barracks. We waited there for two days without food or water.

Young prisoners wearing the required striped clothing gather behind a barbed wire fence at Auschwitz-Birkenau.

First we worked at the camp itself. The guards told us that young workers could volunteer to work in German factories making munitions [ammunition] and other items. Those who went there were promised better food. At dinner, you got a small piece of bread with a little bloodwurst. The bloodwurst was made from parts of the pigs' ears, tails, and fat mixed with pigs' blood in the form of a gel. Many of the inmates were Jews from Kosher* homes. Eating any form of pork was against their religion and they had never done so. These workers wasted away even quicker than the others.

But it was hard to survive on the amount of food any Jewish worker received. My weight dropped from 130 pounds [59 kilograms] to about 90 pounds [41 kg]. Many days I had no hope left. Everywhere I looked I saw terrible things. The Nazis took one block of inmates that was infested with lice and burned them alive.

There was no way out. There were armed guards in towers overlooking the camp. There were also electric fences surrounding the camp. Some inmates committed suicide by throwing themselves against the fences. They couldn't go on anymore. While we were there, we saw German pilots drop leaflets from planes. The leaflets said something like, "Hitler is winning the war, and the Jews will soon all be gone." We had no idea that it wasn't true. It just added to our hopelessness.

---

*Food prepared according to Jewish dietary laws

Though emaciated and weakened, Allan Berk survived about a year and a half at Auschwitz. In the summer of 1942, he was taken to a camp known as Buchenwald. There, he was assigned the task of burying the dead in mass graves. After about four months, he was transported to Bergen-Belsen—another Nazi camp. The conditions there were horrendous.

There was a typhus epidemic at the camp, and the people were dying daily. Their bodies were left out covered

Inmates dying of typhus at the concentration camp Bergen-Belsen

*with flies, and the living had to bury the dead. The sanitary
conditions were terrible. There was only one shower for ten
thousand people. It was in a room about 20 feet [6 meters]
long by 20 feet wide, and there was no soap. We never had
time to get clean. You would get wet and then be hurried
out by the guards. The shower was only available every
third day, and many people didn't shower because of the
conditions. The Nazis tried to dehumanize us. Most
inmates were just waiting to die.*

Allan Berk remained at Bergen-Belsen until the end of the
war. "At first my brother and I were not very excited about

Mildred and Allan
Berk today

being freed," he recalls. "We were too sick. We both had typhus and were running very high fevers. I lost all my hair. I recovered, but the important thing is not that I survived typhus. I am a Jew who survived Hitler."

In 1947, Allan Berk arrived in America through the sponsorship of an older brother who had come to the United States before the war. Allan became a butcher, and eventually bought several butcher shops. He met his wife, Mildred, at Coney Island, a seaside resort in New York, and they were married just three days later. It proved to be the right decision. The couple has been married for forty-eighty years, raised a family of four children together, and now have three grandchildren.

Chapter Five
MIRIAM PULWER

MIRIAM PULWER grew up in a Polish town where her father
sold fabrics that were used for wedding dresses, upholstery,
and other items. As a child Miriam had heard of anti-Semitic
acts in other parts of Poland, but she had never experienced
this hatred until the Nazis rose to power.

Miriam's family's apartment was in the area that became
the ghetto, after the Germans invaded Poland. So they were
allowed to remain there, though they were no longer permitted to come and go freely. In September 1942, the ghetto was
emptied. Its occupants were taken to the railroad station and
loaded into cattle cars.

Miriam Pulwer

We knew that the train was headed for the Nazi death camp Treblinka. There was a broken window on the train and three people in our car said they were going to try to jump out once it was dark. I was friendly with them. Two were Christians married to Jews. My parents told me to go with them. They wanted me to have a chance to live.

We jumped together, but I was soon recaptured when we were stopped at a German checkpoint. The soldiers there didn't know we jumped from a train. They knew I was a Jew because I was the only one still wearing the yellow Star of David that all Jews had to wear. I was put in another cattle car and taken to the Warsaw Ghetto. Now I was alone, but I was glad to be alive. I found out later that the rest of my family died at Treblinka.

The Nazis needed laborers. In Warsaw, I was put to work making brooms. Others in the ghetto made different things like clothes or ammunition. We worked through 1942. We had to work hard. I wasn't alone anymore. My aunt and cousin lived in Warsaw, and I found them in the ghetto.

Jewish men and women are forced to make soles for Nazi shoes in the Warsaw Ghetto.

In January 1943, they started to take people out of the ghetto. We knew they were going to the death camps, so I hid with some others in one of the bunkers that some of the Jewish men had dug beneath the factories. One of the men told me that the sewer connected to the bunker led out of the ghetto to the Gentile part of Warsaw. I decided to try this way out.

I was with some other young people. We hoped we could escape, but when we lifted up the manhole cover on the other side, the Germans were waiting for us. They didn't kill us. We were told that because we were young we would be put to work. We were held at SS* headquarters that night. The next morning we were taken to a railroad station. We were there a day or two before being put into cattle cars.

The train stopped at Majdanek. Oh, what went on there. In the morning, we had to line up and report for roll call. They made selections in the mornings and during the day. People were gassed and put in crematoriums.** It was horrible to know that all around you bodies were burning. Some days I hid in the barracks to miss roll call. I don't know how I stayed alive. I was frightened, but I never stopped wanting to live.

Every day I pulled heavy wagons filled with dirt. There was no purpose to this. We weren't building anything. The Germans just wanted to wear us down, to work us to death.

---

*An elite military group of the Nazis
**Where the dead bodies were burned

Many Jewish people were murdered in this gas chamber at Auschwitz-Birkenau.

There was never very much to eat. In the morning, we got a small piece of bread and butter, and coffee. I never liked butter so I traded it for another small piece of bread. For dinner we had watery soup and a little horse meat. That was it. I arrived at Majdanek in May 1943 and was there for about three months, until August 1943.

By August 1943, the Nazis had begun to empty Majdanek. Many inmates were killed. Others were sent to different camps. Miriam was taken to the Nazi death camp Auschwitz-Birkenau, where she saw the infamous Nazi doctor Josef Mengele. Mengele conducted inhumane medical experiments on Jewish prisoners and called his experiments "scientific research." He also determined, along with other Nazis, which prisoners would live and which would die on any given day.

I saw Dr. Mengele as soon as I got off the train. He could send you to your death then and there. We had to undress right away. The guards searched us to make sure

Dr. Josef Mengele is known as the "Angel of Death" because of his inhumane and fatal experiments on prisoners.

we weren't hiding any valuables. Then they cut our hair and sent us to the showers. When we came out, they tattooed numbers on our arms.

I was taken to Block 103. At first, we just sat in the barracks. Then after about a week, they started calling numbers out. About two hundred people were called to work in munitions. I was one of them. Our living and working areas were filthy. There were lice everywhere, and after about three weeks I started to break out with large boils. I also became extremely ill. Some days my temperature must have been about 103 or 104 degrees Fahrenheit [39 degrees Celsius].

The woman in charge of our block under the Kapo* was a very nice lady. She was Czechoslovakian. She was very kind to me. She told me to stay in bed. I still went out for roll call every morning but then I went back in. I didn't have to go to work. One day she said to me, "You know, you have to go out of the barracks. They are going to clear out all the people in the barracks. You have to go to the hospital."

I did what she said. I went to the hospital. There were

---

*Kapos were also inmates, but they and their assistants were given more privileges in return for keeping the other prisoners under control and seeing that the camp ran smoothly. Some Kapos were Jewish; others were Christian sent to the camp for an assortment of reasons. Though many Kapos were reportedly as brutal as the Nazis, others tried to help the prisoners as much as they could under the circumstances.

Jewish doctors there to take care of the patients, but they had no medicine or supplies. Prisoners either got better or they died. I was there for about three months. Being in the hospital didn't mean I was safe. Every day there were selections. If they called out your number you had to go. Sometimes I hid under the bed to escape them. That would not always work though. You never knew when the Germans would bring in dogs to sniff out those who hid.

The Germans used all kinds of tricks. Sometimes they would call out a number and put that person in a good place. They didn't want us to know what they were doing. That way the inmates would not be able to outsmart them. One day we heard that there was going to be an especially large selection. I went to the Czechoslovakian woman under the Kapo and asked her what I should do. She told me to go to roll call and turn around very fast when they examined me. That was so they would not have very much time to notice my boils and what poor health I was in.

Afterwards, the Kapo's assistant asked me if they wrote down my number after examining me. I told her they had and she told me that she thought that was good. It was good. In the end, my number was the only one called out. I was sent to work in ammunitions. The others there that day were gassed. Their bodies were taken to the crematoriums. When they called your number, you never knew whether you were going to live or die. That's how it was.

At the end of December 1944, or maybe it was January, Auschwitz-Birkenau was closing down.* We were taken on a death march to Ravensbruck, a camp north of Berlin. It was freezing cold. There was ice on the ground and it was slippery. If you fell behind or if you couldn't walk anymore, a guard would shoot you. We weren't given anything to eat as we walked. Many people died along the way. It took about a week to get there. We had to walk most of the way there. They only put us on trains for the last part of the journey. I still had the boots I had come to Auschwitz with and that helped a little. I was at Ravensbruck for three weeks. Then we were moved again.

The Allies were closing in and the Nazis were hurriedly closing camps and moving prisoners from place to place. By now they knew that Germany couldn't possibly win the war and their tightly woven organization had begun to unravel.

We were put on a train to Nordstat, another camp. I was there for two or three weeks until the Allies liberated us. The Americans came in first. They were there for about twenty-four hours before the Russians arrived. We suffered when the Americans left. The Russian soldiers raped a lot

---

*The war was drawing to a close and the Germans knew the Allies were getting close. Not wanting to leave any proof of their atrocities, they were shutting down the death camps.

Prisoners cheer as they are liberated from a Nazi concentration camp.

of the women. I put a compress on my head and began
moaning. They thought I was sick and left me alone.

This was in May 1945. I met my husband after the war.
A Jewish organization helped us get to the United States.
I had a son and a daughter and now I have four
grandchildren. A lot has happened since I was just a girl

in Europe. Yet those memories don't go away. I think about the Holocaust night and day.

Once in the United States, Miriam and her husband bought and ran a restaurant where they served Kosher food. Miriam Pulwer has remained active in various Jewish organizations.

Chapter Six
RUBIN AND GENIA OFFENBACH

RUBIN OFFENBACH grew up in a Polish town known for its anti-Semitism. As a boy, he was frequently beaten up or called names because of his religion. Shortly before the Nazi invasion, his family moved to another part of Poland, thinking they might be safer—but they still weren't safe. Rubin describes the widespread attitude toward Jews at the time: "All of Poland was rife with anti-Semitism."

After the German army arrived in a particular town, all the Jews were ordered to assemble in the market square. They were surrounded by German soldiers pointing machine guns at them. Rubin remembered that the officer in charge told them, "You Jews, as of now, you are considered subhuman."

Rubin and Genia Offenbach in Germany after the war

Sadly, as the weeks and months passed, that's how the Jewish population was treated.

Because he was young and strong, Rubin was not sent to the gas chambers. Instead, he was put to work by the Nazis. One of the camps where he was sent to work was Jaworzno. He labored as a coal miner there for eighteen months. Rubin describes his conditions:

There were about one hundred boys. We walked from the camp to the coal mine in chains. A bunch of prisoners were handcuffed to a rod with a padlock on it; it was easier for the Germans to transport us that way. They only needed about four or five guards. Throughout the year we wore the thin-striped uniforms and wooden shoes we had from another Nazi camp. The summer was better than the winter for us because if someone fell on the snow and ice in those wooden shoes, the whole row of prisoners fell with them. The work was hard. If somebody died in the coal mine we had to carry the body back.

Rubin's experiences at the hands of the Nazis did not end with the coal mine. He also survived several other camps and two death marches. He describes the march from Auschwitz to Buchenwald as follows:

We marched in the dead of winter. If you had to relieve yourself and you didn't get up in time, or if you fell in the snow and didn't get up right away, you were left behind.

There was always a German soldier at the back of the line who finished off the stragglers with a pistol. There were many marches like ours. Bodies were left all over Europe.

Rubin was in a Nazi camp on May 8, 1945, when the Russians came in to liberate the prisoners.

Russian tanks came to the gate. A colonel told us, "You are free, the war has ended." Some of the young men in the camp spoke Russian and one of them told him, "We don't need your freedom, we need food." The colonel understood. He said, "I'll be back in thirty minutes." A half hour later, truck after truck came in with food. They gave us bread and soup. Others, freed by the Americans, were given plenty to eat, and some died because their malnourished bodies couldn't properly absorb the food. I lost a cousin that way.

After the war, Rubin returned to the town in Poland where his family had lived. He didn't know what had happened to his family, and it was there he learned that early in the war the Germans had gassed them in trucks using exhaust fumes. Of the 50 Jewish girls who'd lived in the town, only 2 had survived, and out of 150 Jewish boys, only 6 had survived. The remaining young Jewish people decided to stay together in one house for a while.

The war was over and they were supposedly safe. But were they? Rubin relates what occurred: "We were warned by some Gentile friends that the Polish underground was coming to kill Jewish survivors. They didn't want to return the houses and businesses that the Jews left behind. We had to leave town again." They went to a displaced persons' camp in Munich, Germany, where Rubin married a Jewish girl. The couple emigrated to the United States to begin a new life.

This displaced persons' camp in Berlin had 7,200 people living there, including 525 children without parents.

Rubin's wife, Genia Offenbach, endured a great deal during the war as well. She had also been forced to work in a labor camp, spending about a year and a half on a farm harvesting crops. She describes her experience:

We stayed in the barracks. We had to work until it got dark without rest or breaks of any kind. I saw girls who weren't working fast enough get shot. They would quickly kill you for other infractions too. If you picked up a raw potato to eat, you could be severely beaten.

Her introduction to the Nazi death camp Auschwitz was even worse:

We were assigned our barracks. Mine was near the crematorium. I saw bodies being taken there on my first day at the camp. Some of the friends I didn't see, I later learned, had been gassed. I never expected to see anything like this. In spite of the hard work and brutality at the labor camp, I thought we would be sent home after the harvesting time. I had heard rumors about Jews being killed and their bodies burned. I always thought these were just wild rumors.

When we witnessed the bodies, the fire and smoke, and the smell of the burning bodies, I couldn't eat. I cried and felt the real horror of the situation. The Germans kept up their deception at every turn. As people marched into the gas chamber, they had music piped through the

Bodies were cremated in these ovens.

loudspeaker. They wanted the people to feel safe to make it easier to kill them. Of course, once a person was in the shower, the doors were tightly sealed, and it was too late.

After coming to the United States, Rubin worked in a carpet store and eventually started his own carpet business. Genia worked at home raising their four daughters. Today,

Rubin and Genie Offenbach (center) and their four daughters

the Offenbachs have eight grandchildren. The couple often speaks about the Holocaust. They were honored in May 2000 at a candlelight ceremony in observance of Yom Hashoah, the Day of Remembrance, at the Holocaust Memorial in Miami Beach, Florida.

Chapter Seven
RABBI ANDREW PALEY

THE MARCH OF the Living is an international program through which Jewish high school juniors and seniors from all over the world have an opportunity to visit Poland and Israel and gain a better understanding of the Jewish experience before and after World War II. It is a two-week program—one week is spent in Poland, the other in Israel.

In Poland, the students visit many historic sites to get a feel for what Jewish life was like before Hitler's rise to power. They realize that prior to the Nazis, there had been a Jewish presence in Poland for more than a thousand years. They also visit the Nazi death camps to understand the atrocities that took place during the Holocaust.

Chaperons and Holocaust survivors accompany the stu-

77

Students from all over the world attend the March of the Living program.

dents on the trip. Six months prior to the trip, everyone meets and the students spend some time learning about the Holocaust. This makes their experiences more meaningful.

The program is called the March of the Living because the students actually retrace the steps of concentration camp inmates on the mile-and-a-half walk from Auschwitz to the gas chambers at Birkenau. It was a death march for those who walked it during the Holocaust. The living now take the same journey to honor all who perished at the hands of the Nazis.

Rabbi Andrew Paley describes the purpose of the march: "It's in remembrance of who the victims were, and it's a very powerful time."

Rabbi Andrew Paley has participated in the March of the Living program as a chaperon. He describes his experiences:

Our plane landed in Warsaw and we checked into a hotel. We experienced the Warsaw Ghetto by exploring its perimeters. During the trip, we also visited some synagogues. There is only one synagogue in Warsaw today, but before World War II, there were more than three hundred.

In a little town named Lublin, we saw what was once a yeshiva.* Today it's a medical school, but you can see that some of the windows still have the stained glass from when it was a yeshiva. We went on to visit several of the death camps, including Treblinka, Auschwitz, and Majdanek. We took the seven-hour train ride from Warsaw to Krakow.** There were four hundred Jewish young people on the train wearing the March of the Living blue jackets with the yellow Star of David on it.

There were some strange moments when the local people looked at us and wondered what was going on. We had been deliberately shielded from any real contact with the locals. It's no mystery that most of the death camps were

---

*A school for Jewish scholars
**The city Auschwitz was near

in Poland. And though we don't like to think that Poles feel this way, regrettably some anti-Semitism still exists there. Taking that train ride from Warsaw to Krakow was a haunting experience. All these Jews were on a train in Poland going to Krakow. You couldn't help but think about the many Jews who took this ride in cattle cars years ago.

Our tour guide explained that one of the death camps we visited, Majdanek, had been left in working condition by the Nazis. They left without destroying anything, including the circuitry that electrified the fences. Majdanek had one of the first crematoriums, which was supposedly not very efficient. The gas chambers were there too. I had seen black-and-white pictures of places like this, but being there in person—seeing it in color—made it so real. The horror, the sadness of this terrible reality jumps out at you. You cry. You feel exhausted. You are facing a hideous truth.

We spent three days in Warsaw and would spend about a day and a half in Krakow. We usually took buses around the country. There was a survivor on every bus who could answer questions or clarify things.

The death camps are maintained as museums of sorts by the Polish government, but there is a fine line between preserving a death camp and dressing it up. Some of the survivors with us were extremely upset about what they saw. When we went to Auschwitz, the most infamous death camp of them all, there was an attractively decorated souvenir kiosk at the main entrance. You could buy film, postcards, and other items there. Exit signs and railings had

The experience is very intense and emotional for many people.

been placed in the barracks. It was obvious that the camp had been painted and cleaned up for tourism.

The survivors wanted people to see it just as it was when they were there. One woman on the trip became particularly angry when she saw the grassy areas at Auschwitz. She said that if there had been grass at Auschwitz when they were there, they would have eaten it. Now she feared that people seeing the camp for the first time might get the wrong impression of what it was really like.

In any case, our time at Auschwitz had a bizarre quality to it. We were there on the tenth anniversary of the March of the Living—it was also the fiftieth anniversary of Israel's birth. Because of the occasion, the prime ministers of both Poland and Israel were there for a ceremony. Security was exceptionally stringent due to the diplomats' presence that day. Everyone in our group had to wear the March of the Living blue jacket with the yellow Star of David to gain access to the camp. Once you were inside, you couldn't leave on your own. We had to exit as a group. It was so strange. You had this feeling that Jews were being asked to come into this camp again and were not allowed to leave.

We arrived early in the morning to tour the camp, but the march from Auschwitz to Birkenau wasn't until that afternoon. Since we couldn't leave we had to eat lunch there. So all those people ate in Auschwitz with the gallows and crematorium in plain sight. I couldn't eat. It was too overwhelming. Others were affected the same way, I'm sure. It left you with a profound sense of sadness. There was nothing around me that wasn't hard to look at.

Following the ceremony and the march, we went back to Warsaw and left later that night. We'd spend the next week in Israel. I was glad to leave Poland, but I'll be going back this year. I think it's important to visit the camps because the Holocaust marks one of the most significant events in Jewish history. I think Jews have an obligation to go and begin to put together some of the pieces to understand it all. The experience is so overwhelming; the

Six thousand people from forty different countries participated in the march from Auschwitz to Birkenau in 1996.

vastness of it is staggering. You can't get a sense of it from books or movies. Nothing compares with standing in Auschwitz to make you understand what happened.

People who deny that the Holocaust happened also need to visit the camps. No one can dispute that the camps are there now. Some might try to limit the scope of the Nazis' brutality, but the Germans kept perfect records and these are available at a museum in Israel. Numbers were put on the inmates' arms and their names are in the records. These are valid official documents. The Jews of Europe just didn't disappear.

The participants burn candles during The March of the Living program to remember the victims of the Holocaust.

There are lessons that both Jews and non-Jews can learn from the Holocaust. It is important for everyone to speak out against injustices perpetrated on other people. We need to speak out loudly, clearly, and forcefully. During the Holocaust, Danish Jews were saved because the King of Denmark put on the Star of David armband Jews were required to wear. His followers supported him. They didn't see the separation of peoples. They didn't take the attitude, "It's not happening to me so I don't have to say anything." If there had been a vocal and prolonged protest against Hitler's plan, things might have been different, very different.

Epilogue
HOLOCAUST SILENCE: THE AUTHOR SPEAKS

THE HOLOCAUST is a difficult subject both to read and to write about. It's hard to believe that innocent people can be treated so brutally. Holocaust survivors differ in how they feel about discussing their experiences. Many find it too painful. Some of the survivors I contacted did not want to be interviewed for this book. One woman said, "I don't want to talk about the Holocaust. I can't even say the word. I don't want to see my story on paper. I want to leave it behind me, but I don't think I ever will."

Another Holocaust survivor I met worked with survivors at a Holocaust documentation center. Her work focused on recording the events of the Holocaust and the stories of survivors for future generations. When I spoke with her, she mentioned that during the war she was in a ghetto and then a Nazi camp. I asked her to tell her story but she declined, noting that she had not even recorded it for the documentation center where she worked.

I am familiar with the silence of Holocaust survivors and their families. Through the years, I often came across it. I also found the silence in my father.

My father was a Russian Jew who came to the United States before the war. He had come from a very large family, and had been one of two brothers who had escaped the anti-Semitism that prevailed in their homeland. Because we lived in New Jersey and my uncle settled in Cuba, I grew up with a curious lack of cousins on my father's side.

My father was always my favorite parent. He was warm and loving, and I felt I could speak to him about anything—except his family. When I was about seven, I asked him whether he had any brothers or sisters, and he answered yes. When I asked what their names were, he immediately responded, "What does it matter what their names were? They are not here now."

That was the last time he spoke to me about his family. He seemed extremely upset, and that was the harshest tone he ever used toward me. I had unknowingly hit on a very painful wound. The following year, I unintentionally walked in on him as he was saying something to my mother about his sister in Poland. He stopped talking the minute he saw me standing in the doorway. Because of that, I grew up thinking that my father's extensive family was somewhere in Europe

The author,
Elaine Landau

dying of natural causes. Being Jewish, I learned about the Holocaust as a child. Some of my friends had parents who were Holocaust survivors and had lost family members in Europe. I felt connected to those who died. They were Jews—my people—and now they were gone. I never dared think that I was more directly connected to what had happened. I had no idea that Hitler was the reason there were never cousins from my father's side at my birthday parties.

My father died when I was eleven. The time for questions was over, and I still knew nothing about his family. As an adult, I frequently read and wrote about the Holocaust. Nevertheless, it wasn't until last year that I learned the truth about my family.

I had moved to Miami, Florida, and I was reunited with some cousins who had moved there from Cuba. We had much to talk about, and I quickly realized that they were far more knowledgeable about our shared heritage. I asked them about our fathers' family in Europe. Did they ever hear from them? Looking at me incredulously, one replied, "They're all dead. They were killed in the Holocaust." Hearing these words, I felt as if I were on a high-rise elevator that had just crashed to the bottom floor. I said, "I never knew." Yet, at that moment, I realized that somehow I had always known.

I also learned what happened to my father's sister, Sarah—the sister I had heard him talking about. Sarah was an unusually intelligent young woman who had become a dentist. At one point, she was the only dentist in the Polish town of Mir, which had about four hundred residents. Many Jews were killed or sent to labor camps after the Nazi invasion, but Sarah's experience was different. The Germans needed dentists badly, so she was moved to a house in the city's Jewish ghetto where the Germans had also situated a doctor and a pharmacist. There she worked with her husband, Julius, who was a dental technician.

While living in the ghetto, the couple and their son heard rumors. There was talk of Jews being killed in Nazi camps

James K. Garmiza, Elaine's father, stands proud at his poultry farm.

specifically designed for this purpose. The Germans kept the skilled workers alive, but since Julius was considered less essential than his wife, Sarah feared that her husband might be at risk. Fortunately, she found a Christian couple who agreed to hide him in their attic. They had been Sarah's dental patients before the war.

Sarah's son, Jack, was taken in by another Christian family who were also Sarah's former patients. They owned a farm in a secluded part of the countryside and kept Jack safe by dressing him in farm clothes and putting him in the fields with the other farmhands. No one ever guessed that he was Jewish.

Julius and Jack were safe, but in the end, Sarah was not. The Germans may have wanted her alive, but she fell victim to the Polish police, who in some areas were as anti-Semitic and brutal as the Nazis. One evening, they unexpectedly burst into her room, where they robbed and murdered her.

That is what happened to my father's sister—the only sister I ever heard him mention. I often think about what it would have been like to have an aunt. Would she have looked like me? Would we have done things together? I understand Holocaust silence much better now. The loss of family must have been horrendous for my father. I understand why he couldn't talk about it—especially to a small child.

Sarah and millions like her are gone now. All of them are forever lost to their loved ones. Though we want to share our joys and special moments with them, we can never bring them back. We can only try to ensure that the horror and destruction will never happen again to anyone, anywhere.

FOR MORE INFORMATION

Books

Altman, Linda Jacobs. *The Holocaust, Hitler, and Nazi Germany*. Berkeley Heights, NJ: Enslow, 1999.

Ayer, Eleanor H. *In the Ghettos: Teens Who Survived the Ghettos of the Holocaust*. New York: Rosen, 1999.

Bachrach, Susan D. *The Nazi Olympics*. Boston: Little, Brown, 2000.

Brager, Bruce L. *The Trial of Adolf Eichmann: The Holocaust on Trial*. San Diego: Lucent, 1999.

Dvorson, Alexa. *The Hitler Youth: Marching Toward Madness*. New York: Rosen, 1999.

Keelye, Jennifer. *Life in the Hitler Youth*. San Diego: Lucent, 1999.

When I was about four or five I sometimes played with a Christian girl. She lived down the street. She was about two or three years older than me, but we got along very well. We were good friends. One day I happened to mention that I was Jewish. She didn't react one way or another. It didn't seem

Lyman, Darryl. *Holocaust Rescuers*. Berkeley Heights, NJ: Enslow Publishers, 1999.

Mandell, Sheri Lederman. *Writers of the Holocaust*. New York: Facts On File, 1999.

Nardo, Don. *The Rise of Nazi Germany*. San Diego: Greenhaven, 1999.

Newman, Amy. *The Nuremberg Laws: Institutionalized Anti-Semitism*. San Diego: Lucent, 1999.

Nieuwsma, Milton J. *Kinderlager: An Oral History of Young Holocaust Survivors*. New York: Holiday House, 1998.

Opdyke, Irene Gut, and Jennifer Armstrong. *In My Hands: Memories of a Holocaust Rescuer*. New York: Knopf, 1999.

Tito, E. Tina. *Liberation: Teens in the Concentration Camps and the Teen Soldiers Who Liberated Them*. New York: Rosen, 1999.

Wukovits, John F. *Ann Frank*. San Diego: Lucent, 1998.

Websites

ADL online
http://www.adl.org
The Anti-Defamation League is the world's leading organization in the battle against anti-Semitism. This site has information about the group's programs and services.

Cybrary of the Holocaust
http://www.remember.org
This site uses art, discussion groups, photos, poems, narratives, and historic information to preserve memories and educate people about the Holocaust. It includes a forum where users can post memories about victims or survivors.

The Holocaust-History Project
http://www.holocaust-history.org
A free archive of documents, photographs, recordings, and essays regarding the Holocaust.

March of the Living
http://www.motl.org
The official site of the March of the Living program, which brings Jewish youth from all over the world to Poland and Israel to retrace the death march that concentration camp inmates made from Auschwitz to the gas chambers at Birkenau.

United States Holocaust Memorial Museum
http://www.ushmm.org/holo.htm
This site is dedicated to the documentation, study, and interpretation of Holocaust history. It includes online exhibits of art and photos.

INDEX

Italics indicate pages with illustrations.

ABOUT THE AUTHOR

AWARD-WINNING AUTHOR Elaine Landau has a bachelor of arts degree in English and journalism from New York University and a master's degree in library and information science from Pratt Institute. She worked as a newspaper reporter, a children's book editor, and a youth services librarian before becoming a full-time author. Ms. Landau has written more than one hundred nonfiction books for young readers. She lives in Miami, Florida, with her husband, Norman, and son, Michael.

FIELDS CORNER